Puzzle Pals

Drawing With Mom

Drawing With Mom

Bryce Ross

ISBN: 978-1-990100-76-5

www.puzzlepalsbooks.com/kids

@puzzlepals_books

puzzlepalsbooks

This book belongs to

_____

- - - - - - - - - - - - - - - - - - -

_____

SELF PORTRAIT!

Draw a picture of your mom and yourself...

Super Hero Duo!

Draw a picture of the two of you as super heroes...

 # Underwater Adventure!

Draw a picture of the two of you snorkeling under water...

 # Animal Kingdom

Draw a picture of the two of you in the jungle with animals...

Garden Dreamland!

Draw a magical garden with large plants, flowers, and cute creatures...

Space Adventure!

Draw yourselves as astronauts flying through space while discovering planets and aliens...

Fairy Tale Castle!

Build and draw your own castle complete with flags, towers, prince, and princess...

Circus Performers!

Draw yourselves as two circus performers like jugglers or tightrope walkers...

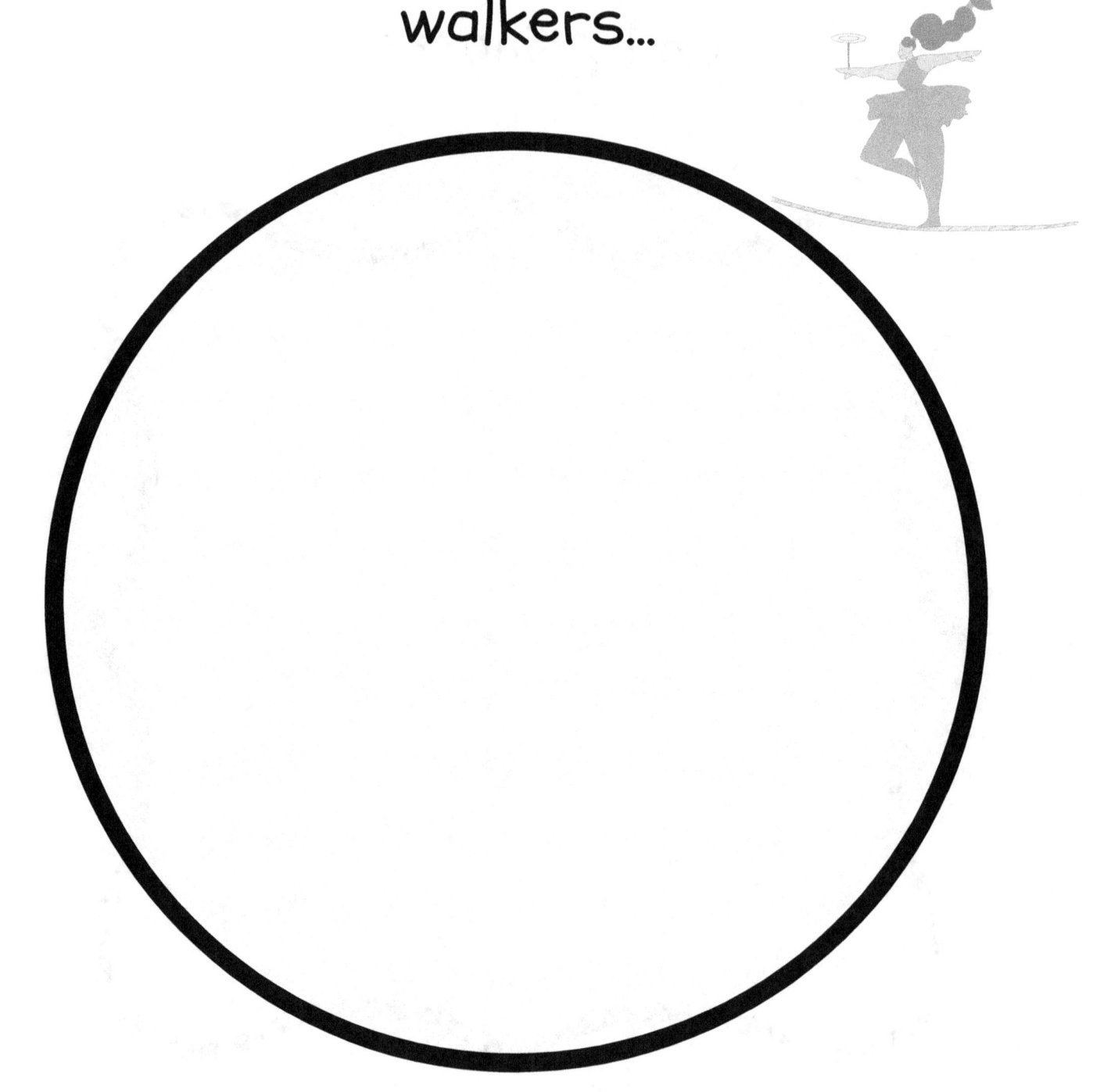

Adventure in the clouds!

Draw yourselves flying in the sky surrounded by clouds and birds...

Safari Expedition!

Draw yourselves on a safari with elephants, giraffes, and other animals...

Time travellers!

Time travel to the future! Draw what you think the future looks like...

Pirate Life!

The two of you are now pirates! Draw yourselves on a pirate ship...

Camping in the Woods!

The two of you are now camping in the woods! Draw yourselves camping under the stars...

Dream Treehouse!

Building time! Draw an amazing treehouse the two of you can play in...

Monster Makeover!

Cute monsters have arrived! Draw some cute monsters you would like to be friends with...

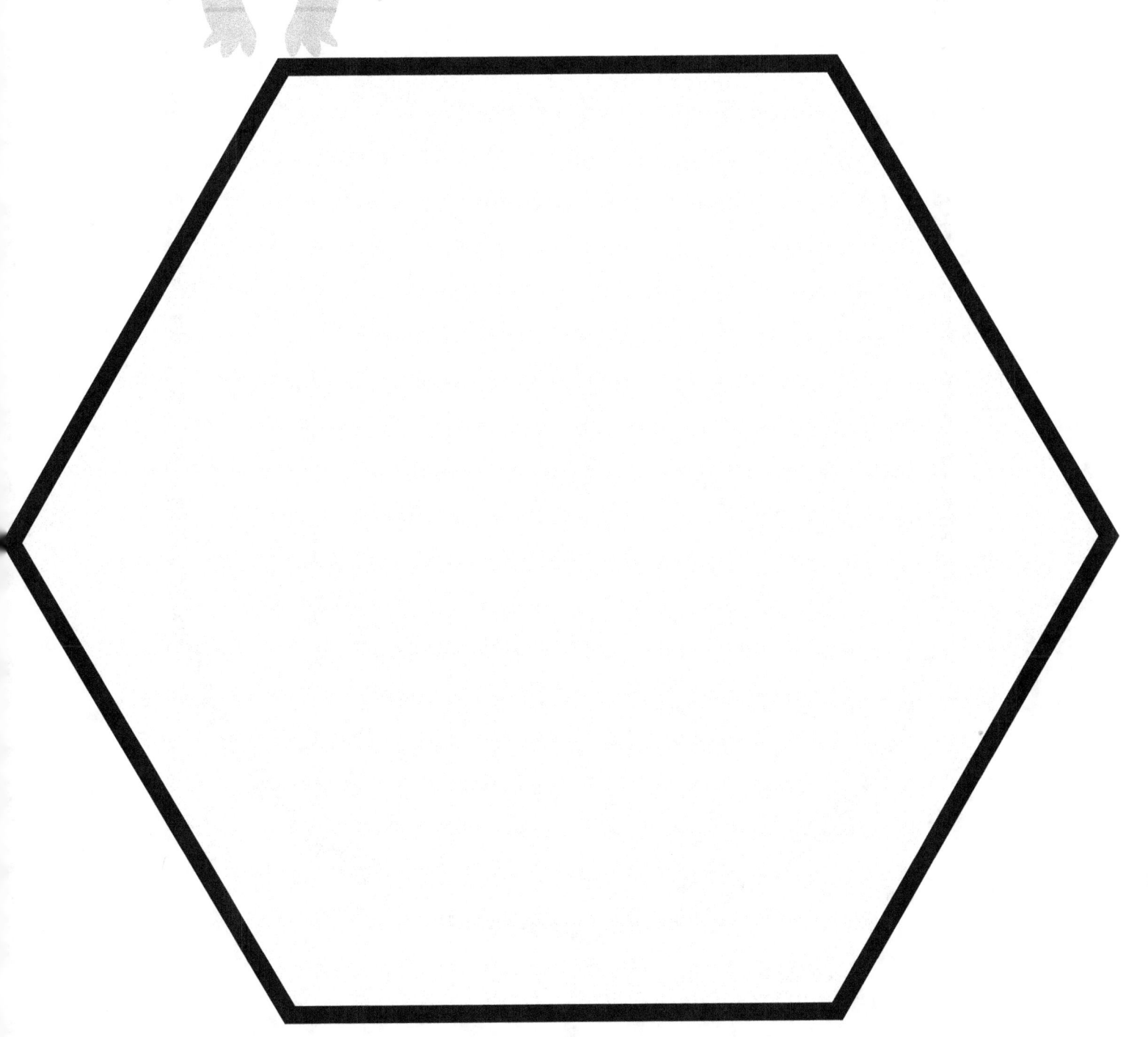

Robot Wrestlers!

Robot wrestling! Draw the coolest robots you can think of...

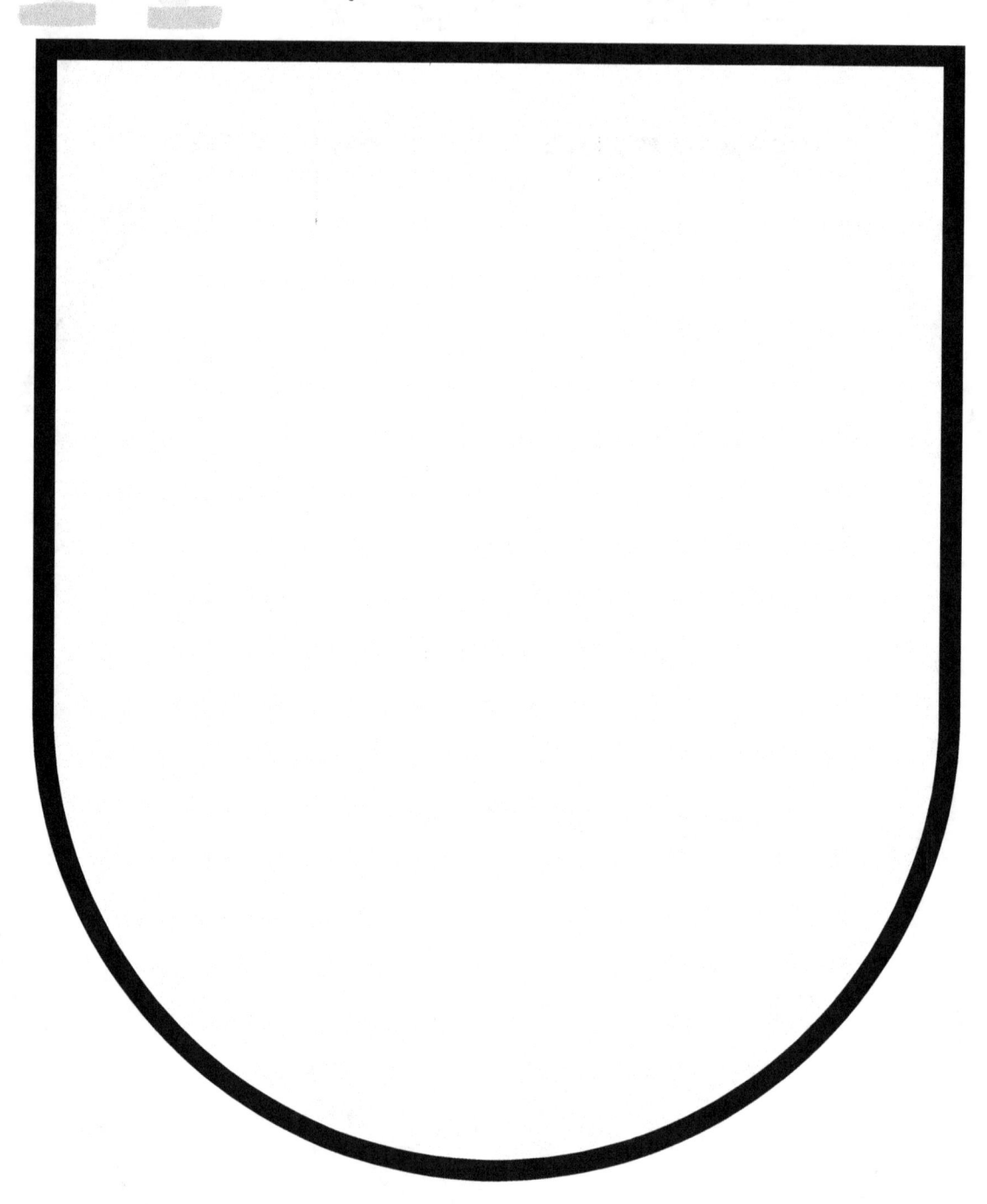

Flying Friends!

It's time to fly! Draw yourselves flying on the back of a magical creature like a unicorn...

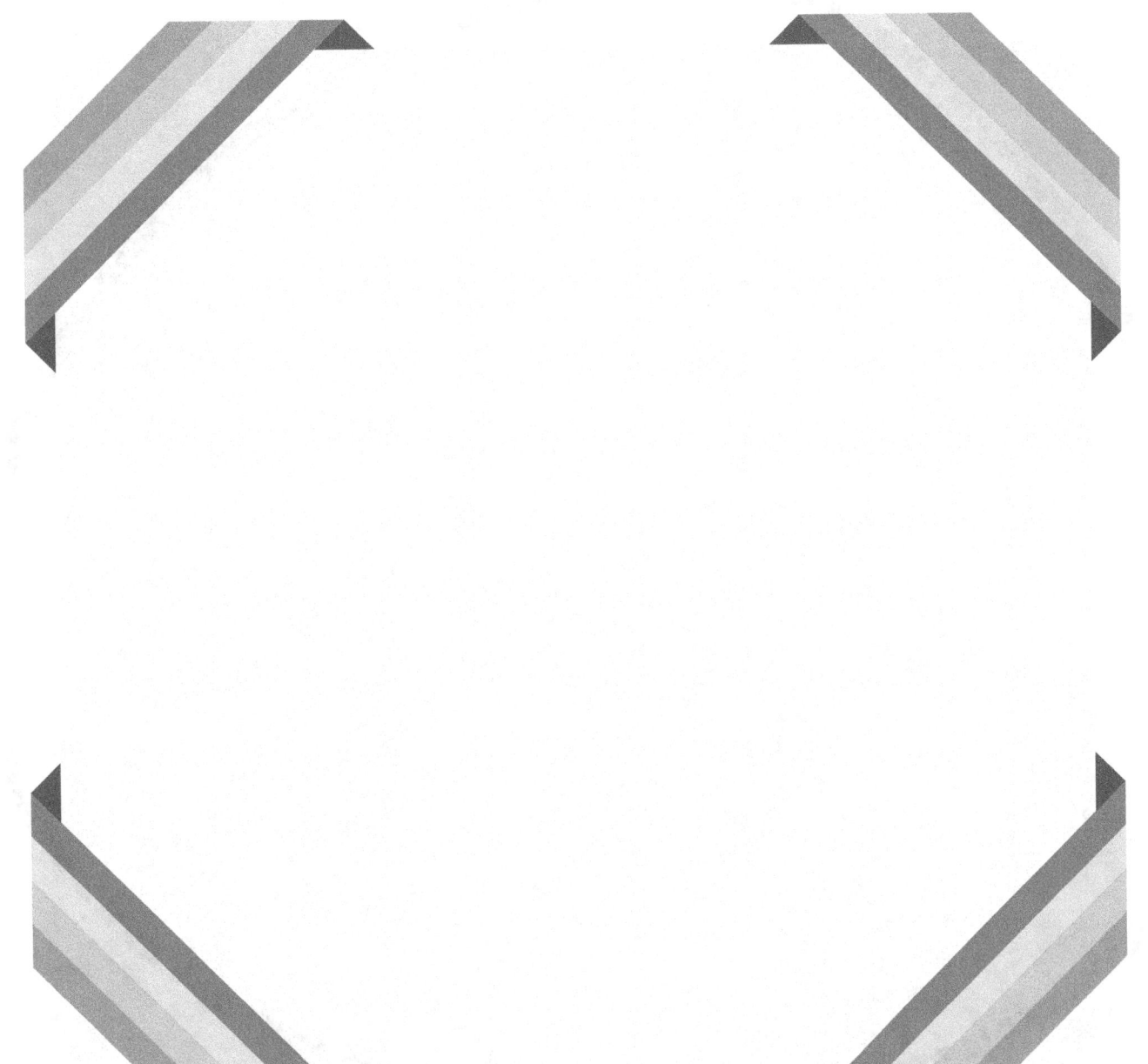

Baker Blast!

Draw yourselves as bakers making the most delicious cakes...

Super Surfers!

Draw yourselves surfing huge waves at the beach...

Cool Cooks!

Draw yourselves as cool cooks making your favorite dinner...

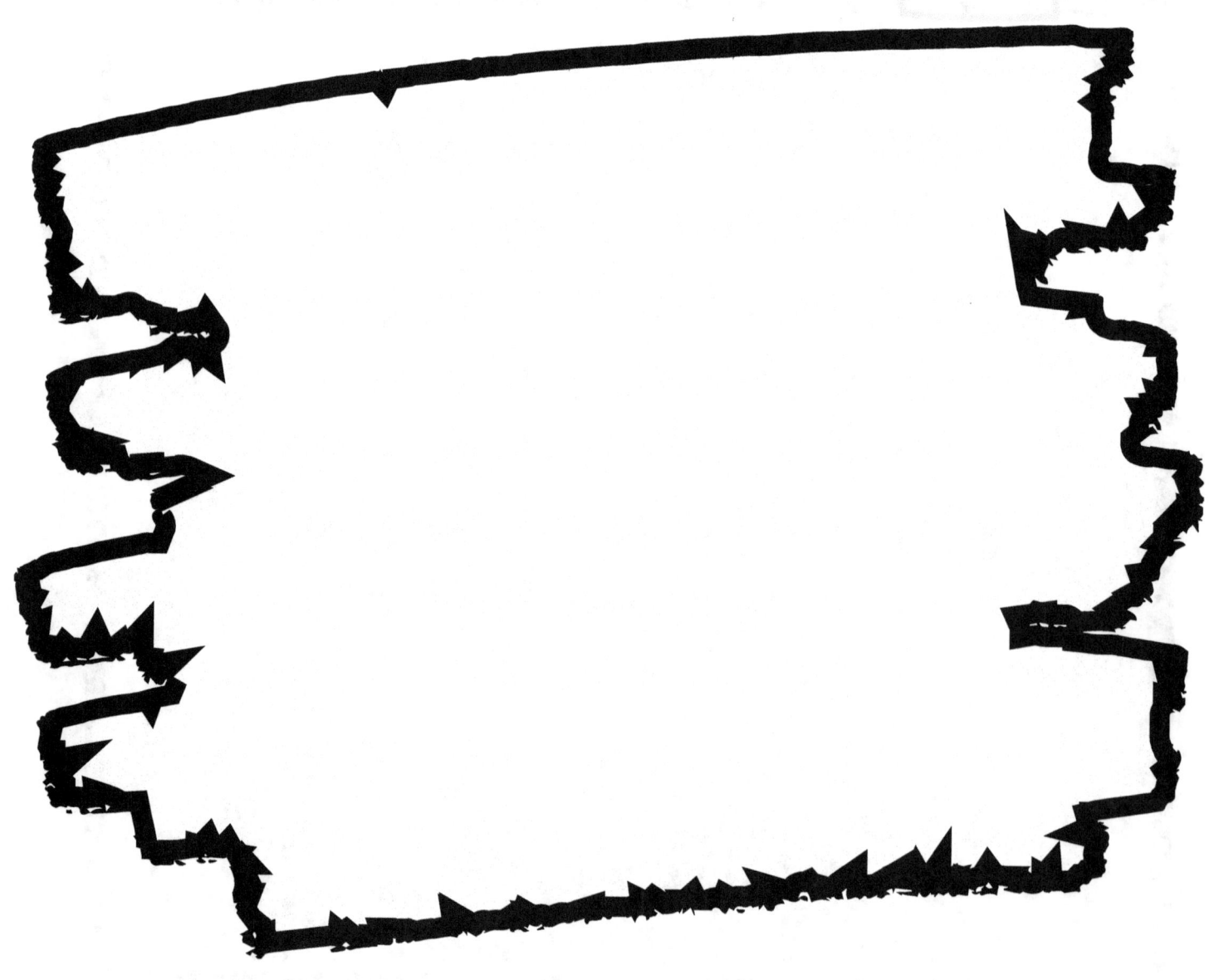

Secret Agents!

Time to save the world! Draw yourselves as secret agents...

Monster Mashup!

Draw big monsters, small monsters, scary monsters, and cute monsters...

Alien Planet!

You've landed your spaceship on an alien planet! Draw the aliens and plants on this planet...

We See Seashells!

Welcome to the beach! Draw seashells, starfish, and crabs...

Favorite Season!

Do you like Fall, Winter, Spring, or Summer? Draw your favorite season...

Dinosaur World!

You've gone back in time! Draw yourselves with dinosaurs...

Fantasy Parade!

Draw a parade with your favorite animals and magical creatures...

Dream Playground!

Time to go to the park! Draw your dream playground with slides and swings...

Magical Forest!

The forest is magic! Draw animals that talk and plants that glow...

Magic World!

The two of you are magic! Draw yourselves completing a spell with your magical wands...

Perfect Pets!

Draw a picture of amazing pets in your house...

Happy Holidays!

Draw a picture of the two of you celebrating your favorite holiday...

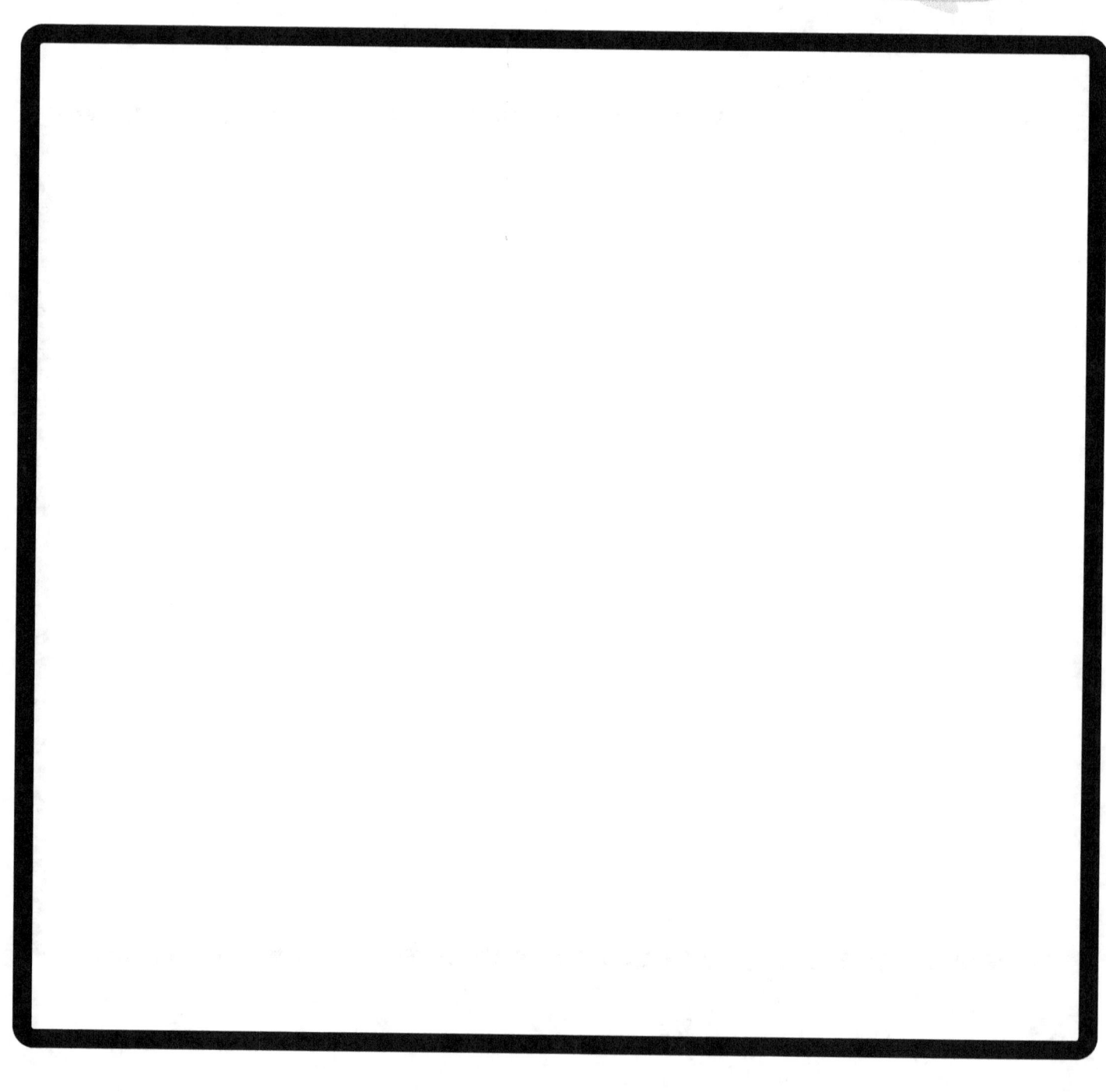

Birthday Bash!

Draw a picture of celebrating mom's birthday...

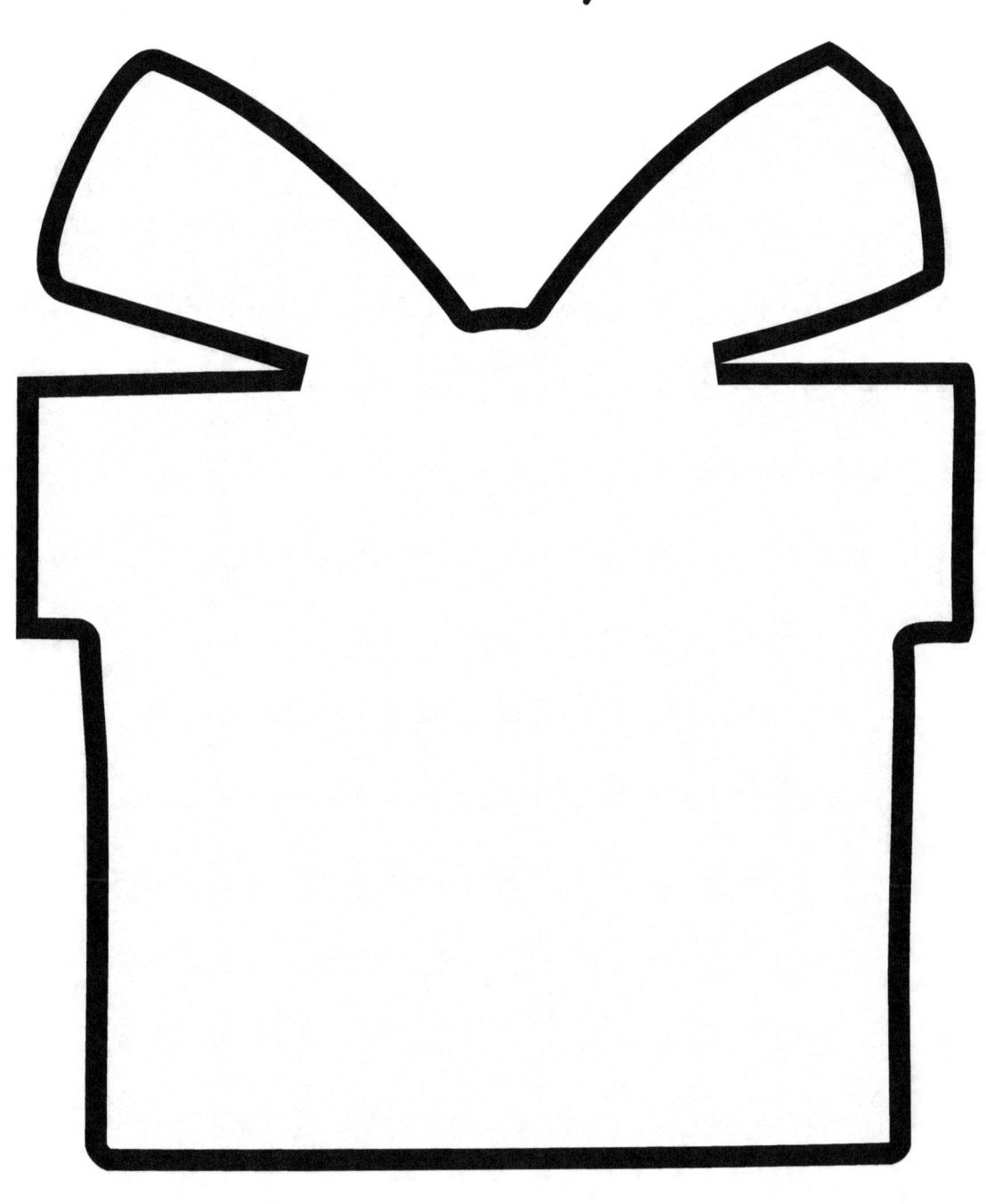

Birthday Bash!

Draw a picture of celebrating child's birthday...

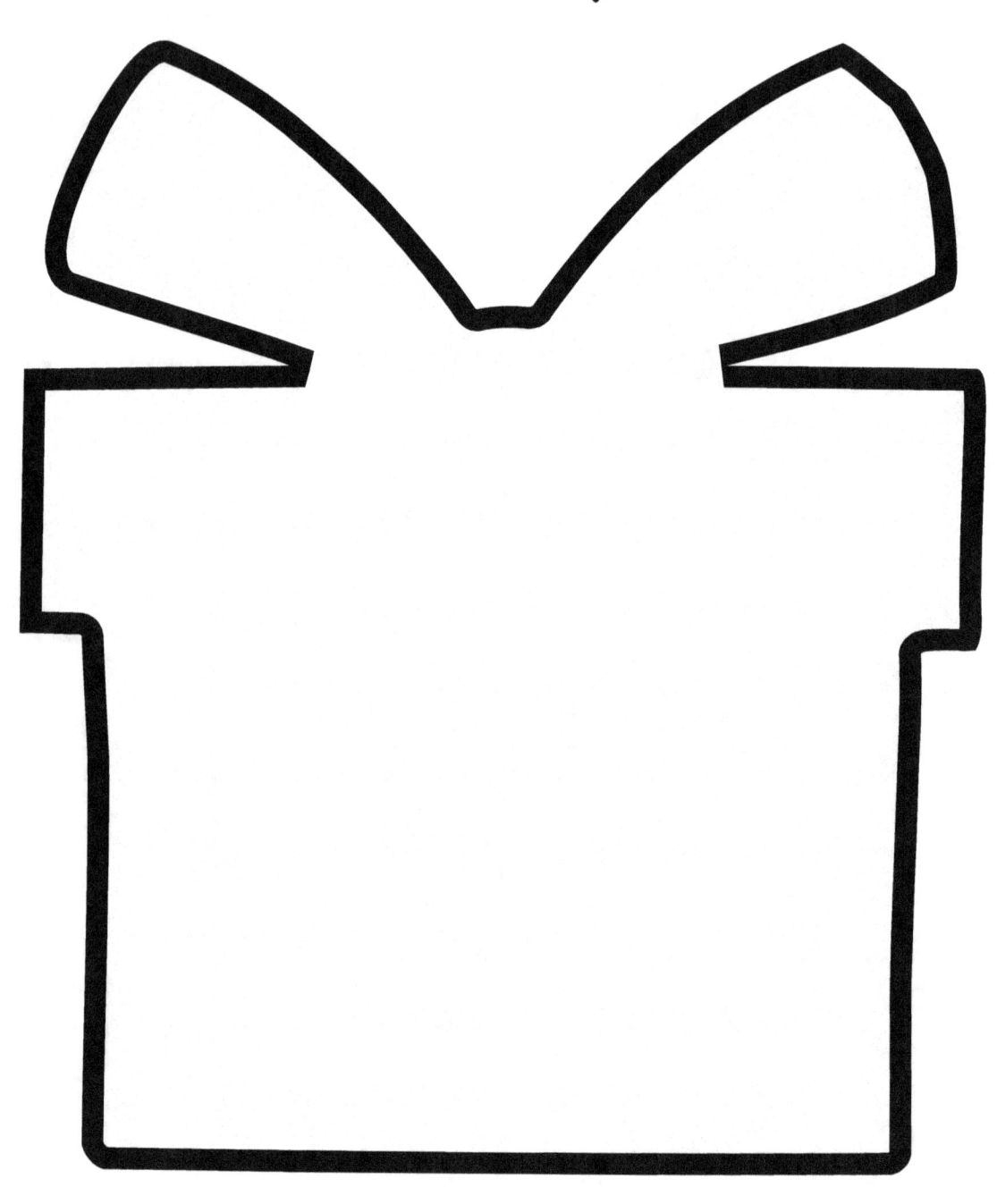

Trick of Treat!

Draw a picture of the two of you in costume on Halloween...

Dream House!

Draw a picture of the perfect 'dream house' for your family...

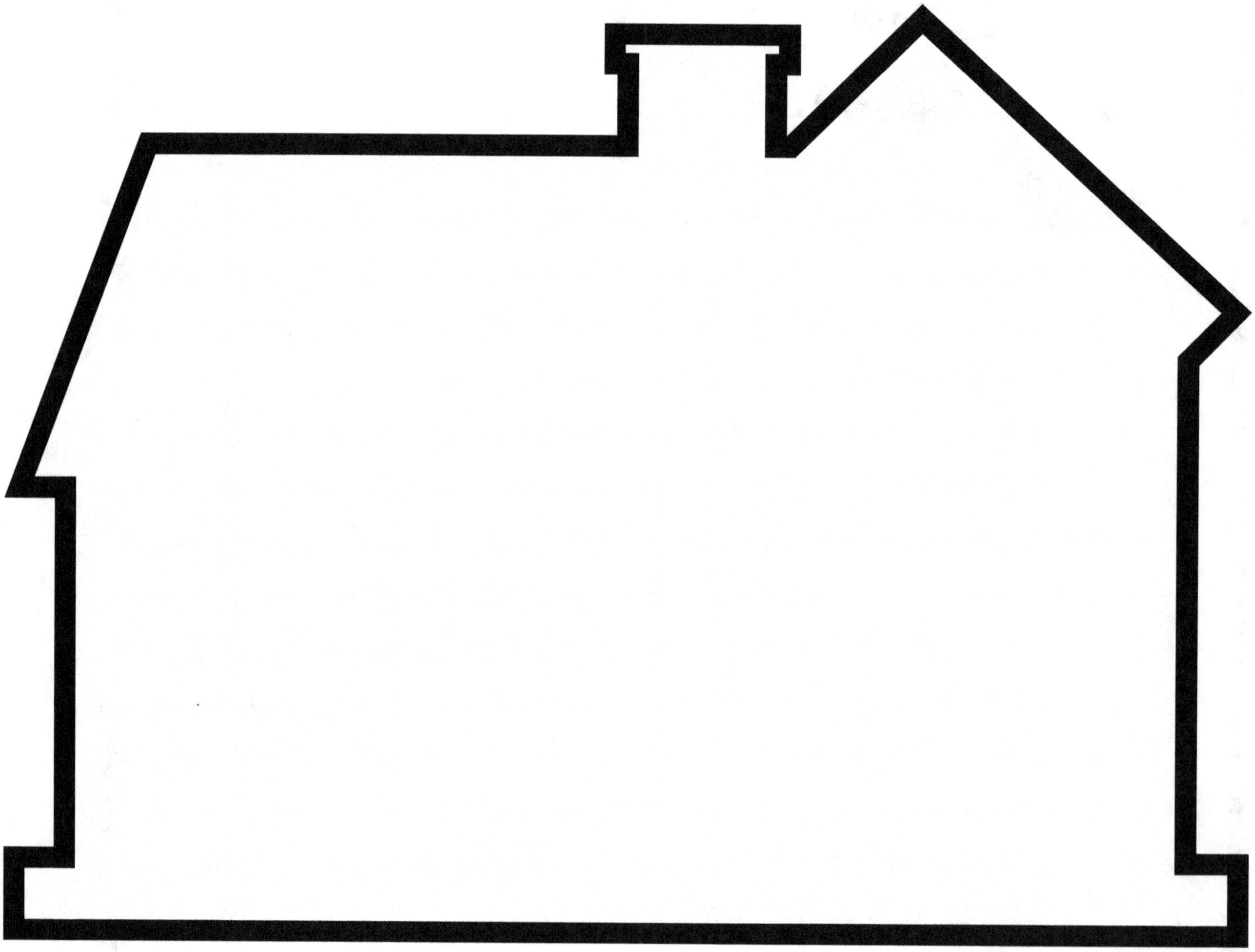

Wild Waterpark!

Draw a wild waterpark with colorful slides and swimming pools...

Winter Wonderland!

Draw yourselves in a 'winter wonderland' with snow flakes and snowmen...

Family Portrait!

Photo day! Draw a picture of everybody in your family...

Hand in Hand!

Trace your hands on this page! Who has a bigger hand???

Farmhouse Fun!

Draw yourselves on a farm! What animals do you see...

Rainbow World!

Draw yourselves underneath a beautiful rainbow...

Flying Cars!

Draw yourselves a flying car to ride in the sky...

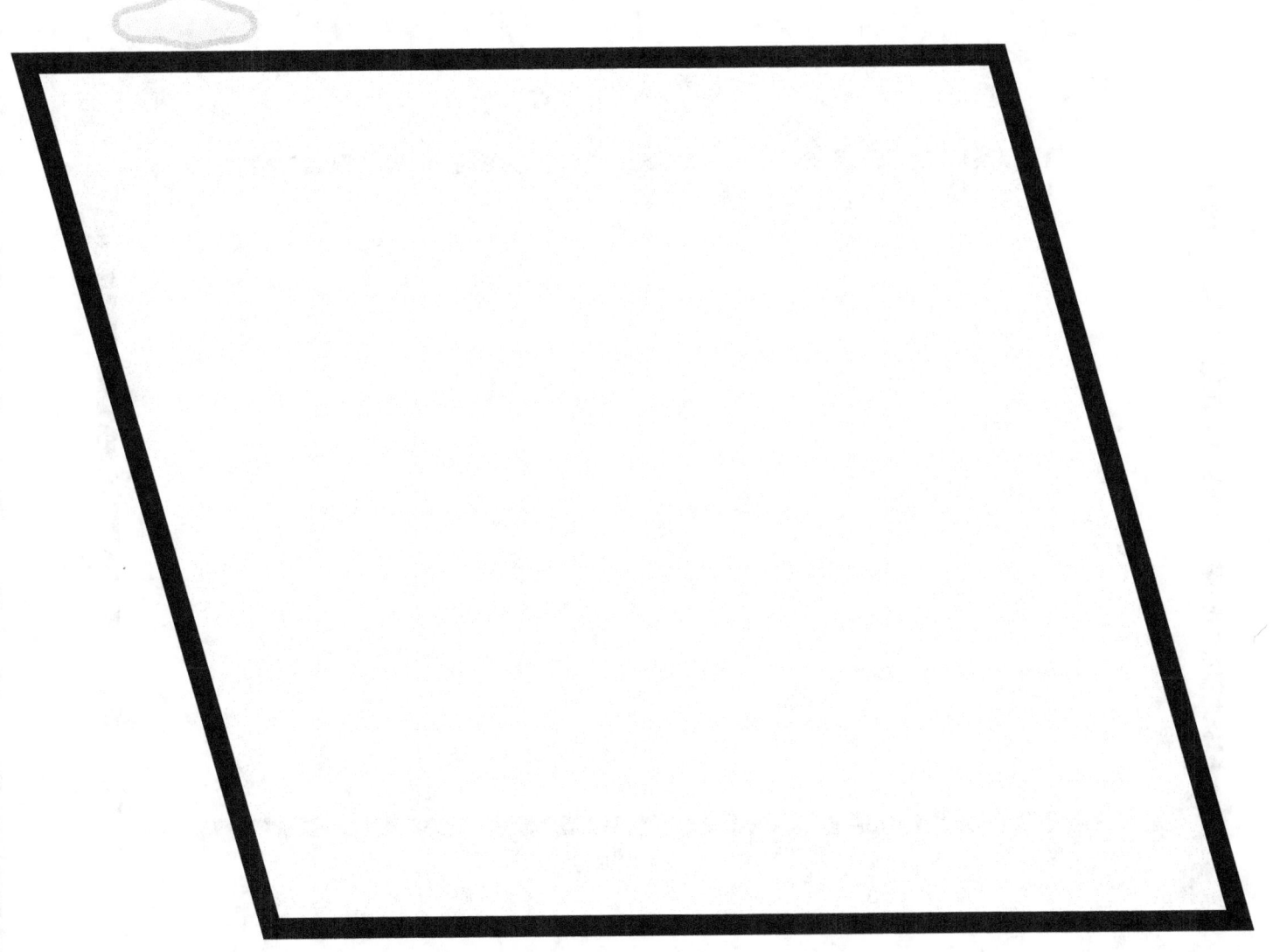

Cute Creatures!

Draw the cutest kittens and puppies you can think of...

Dinosaur Rides!

Draw yourselves riding on top of your very own T-Rex...

Amazing Amusement Park!

Draw your very own amusement park with roller coasters and ferris wheels...

Perfect Pizza!

You two are pizza chefs! Draw the perfect pizza with delicious toppings...

Giant World... Tiny People!

The two of you have shrunk to the size of a finger. Draw the giant world around you...

Underwater Explorers!

Draw yourselves in a submarine underwater... what do you see out the window???

Funny Outfits!

Draw yourselves wearing the funniest outfits you can think of...

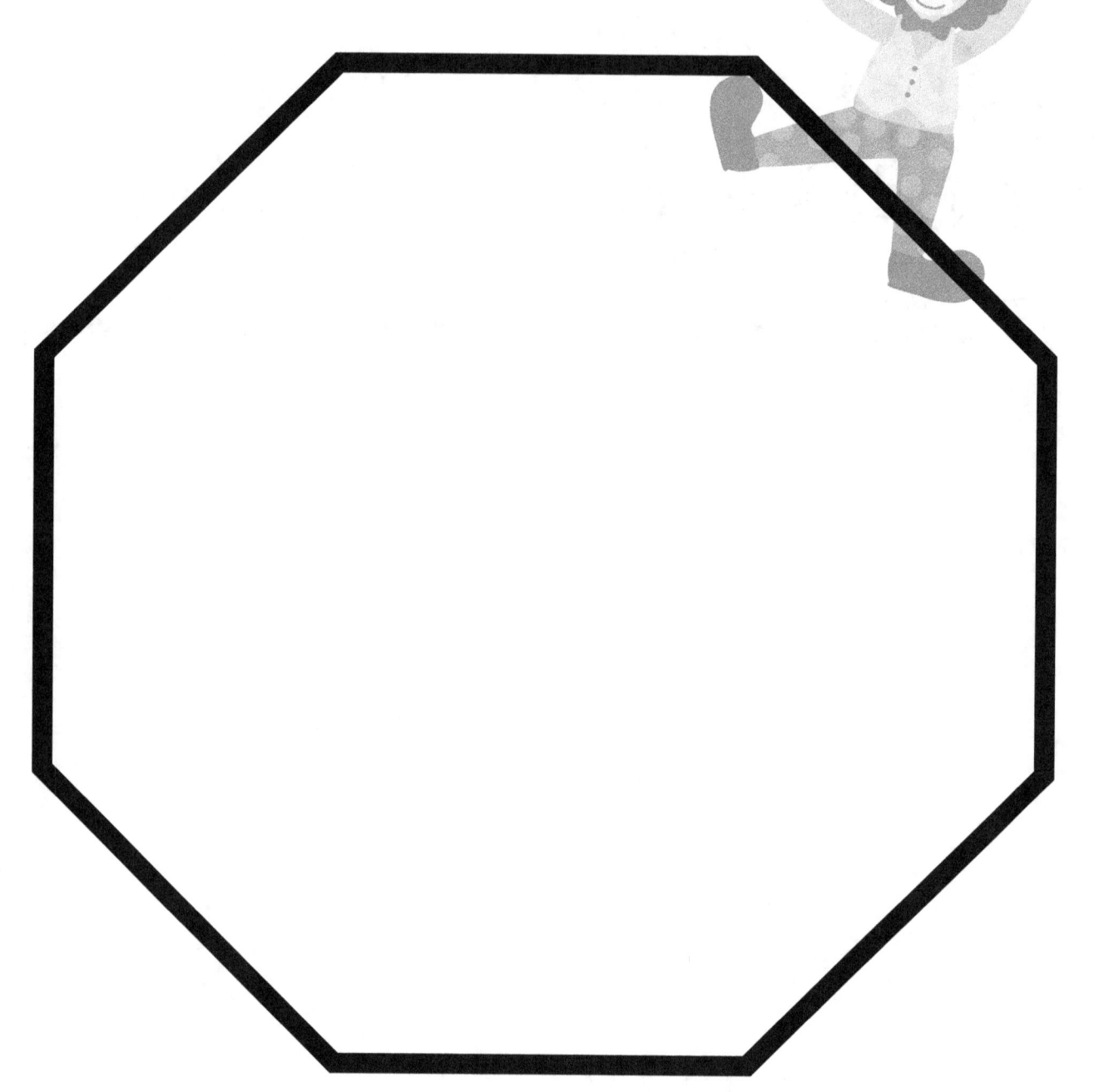

Take Mom to School!

Draw yourselves at school with your favorite teacher...

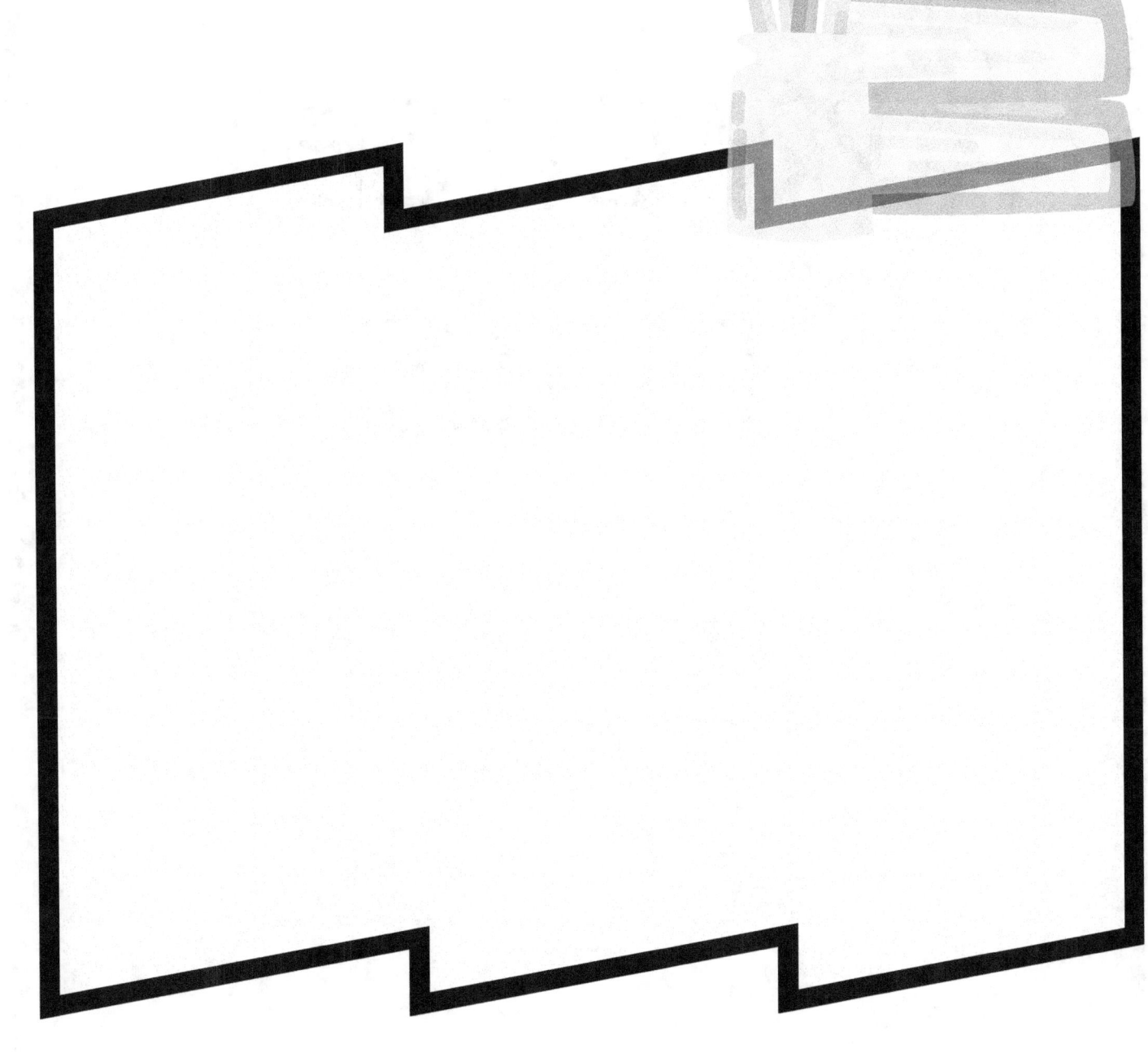

PRACTICE PAGES

PRACTICE PAGES

Kitten

Puppy

Rabbit

Crab

Goldfish

Octopus

Mom Draws

Kitten

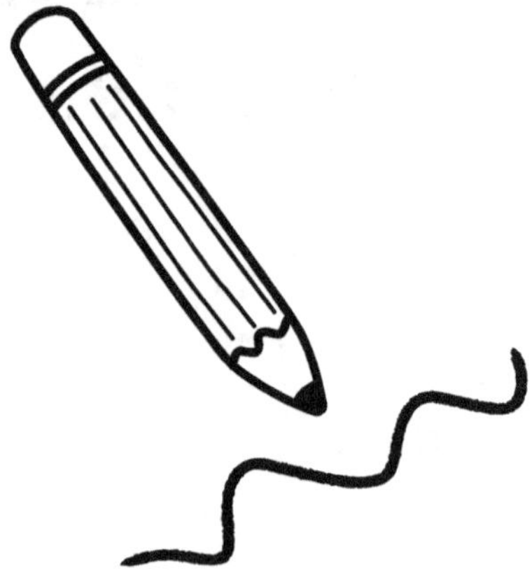

Child
Draws

Kitten

Mom Draws

Puppy

Child
Draws

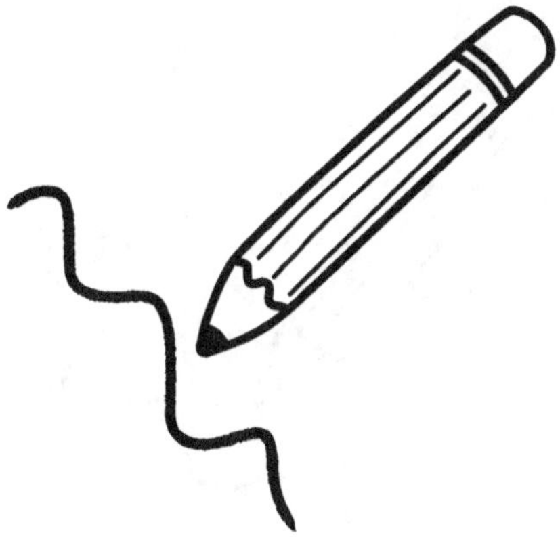

Mom Draws

Child
Draws

Rabbit

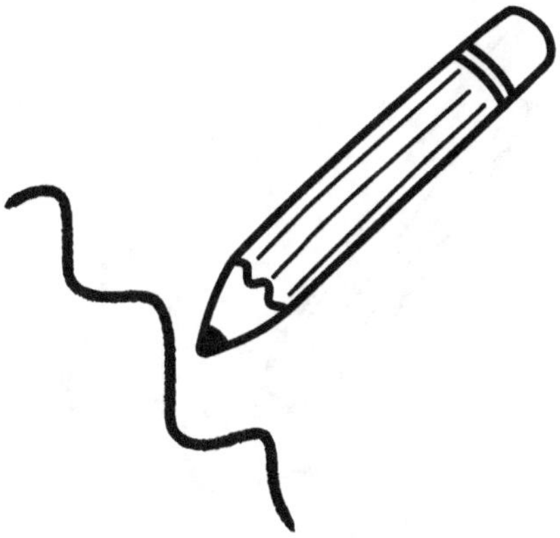

Mom
Draws

Child Draws

Crab

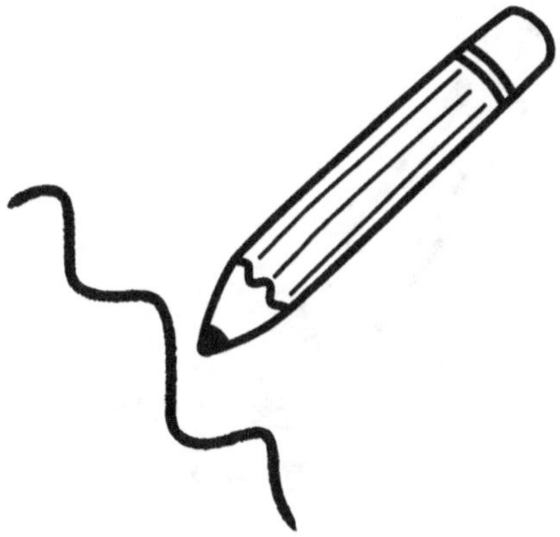

Mom Draws

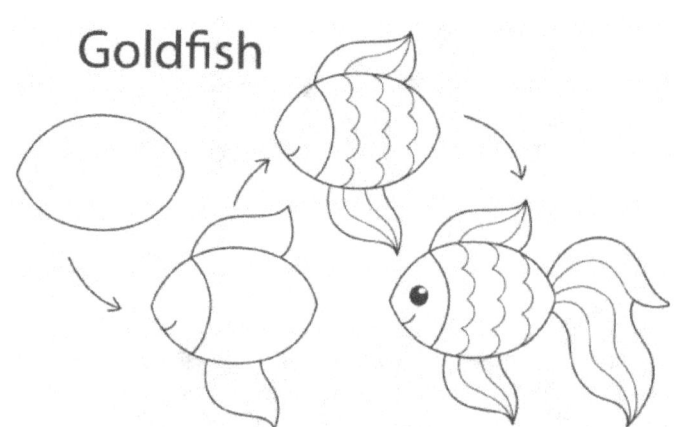

Child

Draws

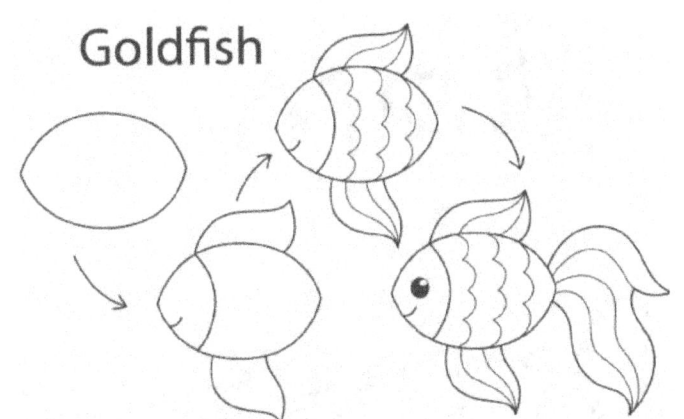

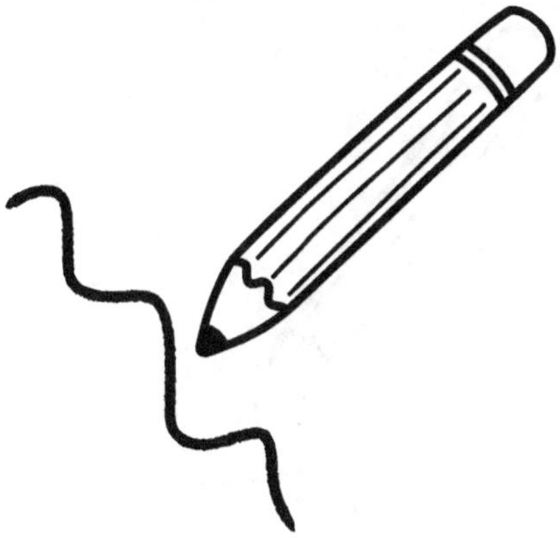

Mom Draws

Octopus

Child Draws

Octopus

Together

Mom draw a house for animals...
Child draw any animals that live
in the house...

Together

Child draw a fish bowl...
Mom draw different sea
animals...

Tiger

Lion

Elephant

Leopard Practice

Giraffe Practice

Hippopotamus Practice

Mom Draws

Child Draws

Tiger

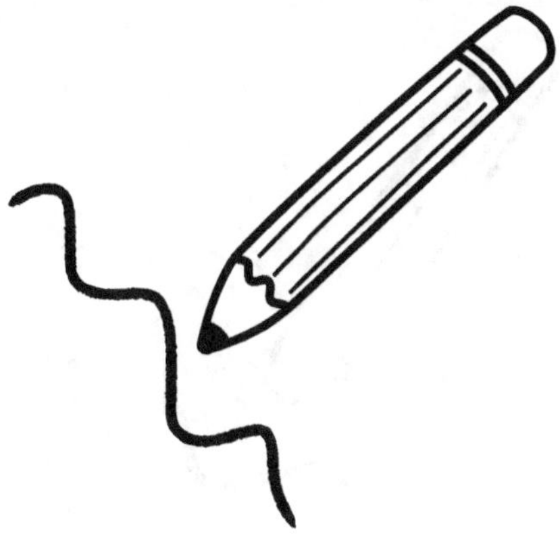

Mom Draws

Lion

Child Draws

Lion

Mom Draws

Elephant

Child
Draws

Elephant

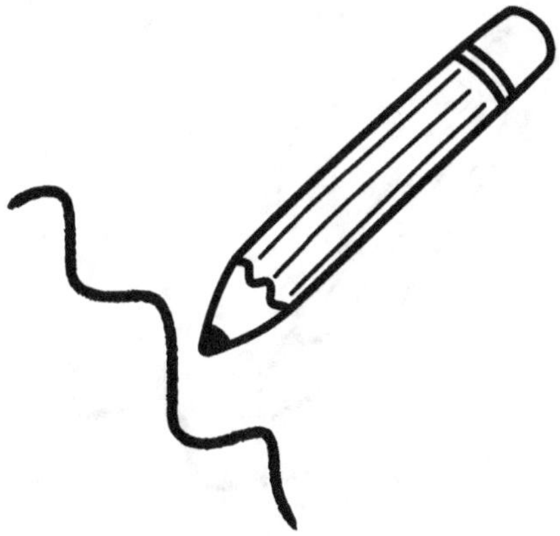

Mom
Draws

Child Draws

Leopard

Mom Draws

Child
Draws

Giraffe

Mom Draws

Hippopotamus

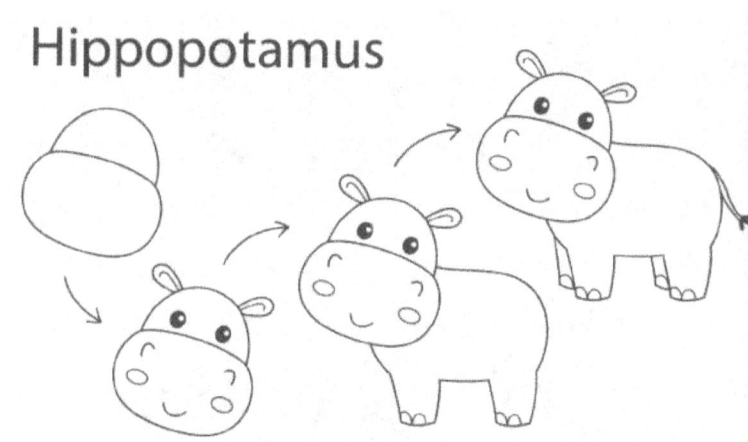

Child

Draws

Hippopotamus

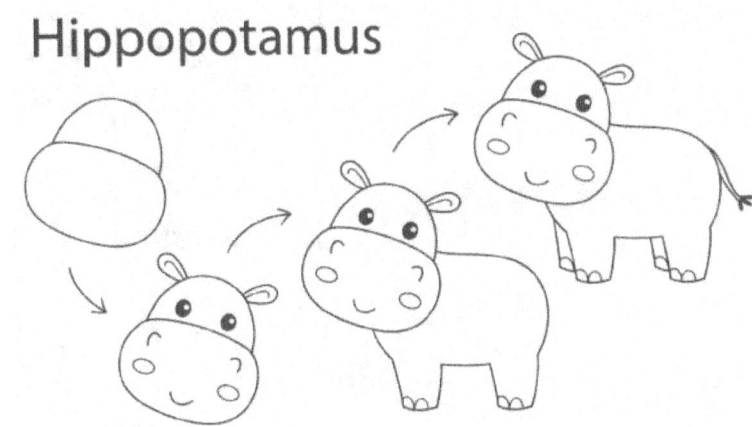

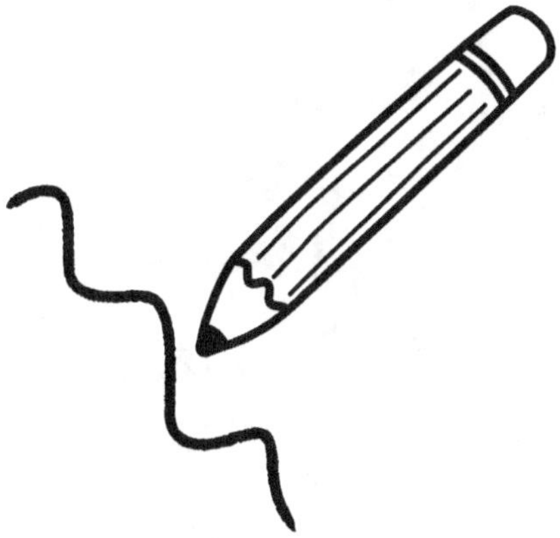

Together

Mom draw trees and plants...
Child draw animals that live
in the jungle...

Together

Child draw your favorite jungle animals...

Mom draw funny hats on the animals...

Dolphin Practice

Shark Practice

Whale Practice

Penguin Practice

Seal Practice

Sea Lion Practice

Mom Draws

Dolphin

Child Draws

Dolphin

Mom
Draws

Child

Draws

Mom Draws

Whale

Child Draws

Whale

Mom Draws

Penguin

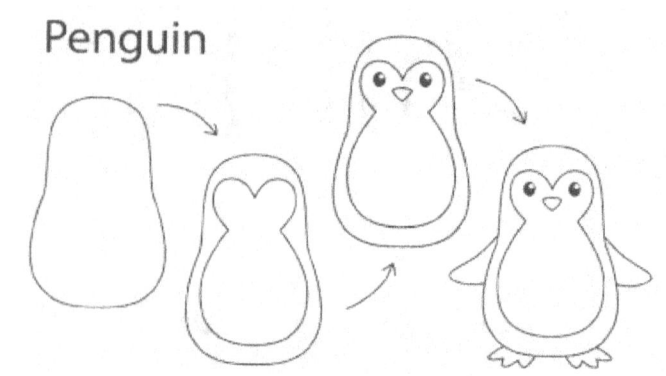

Child
Draws

Penguin

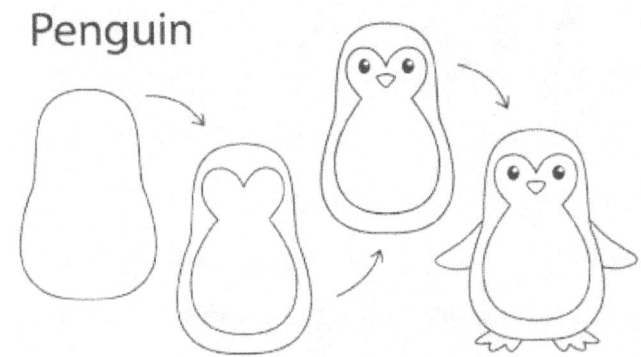

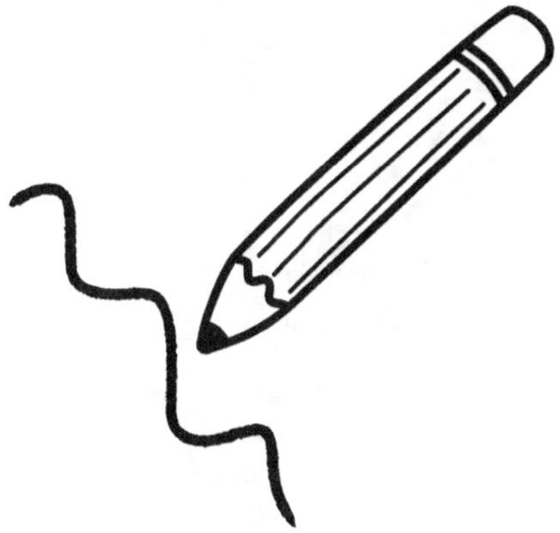

Mom Draws

Child
Draws

Seal

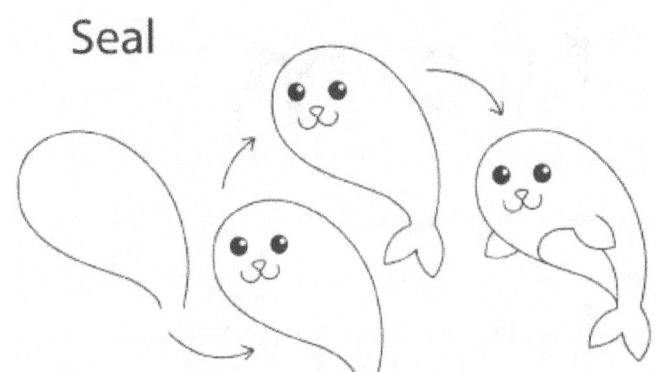

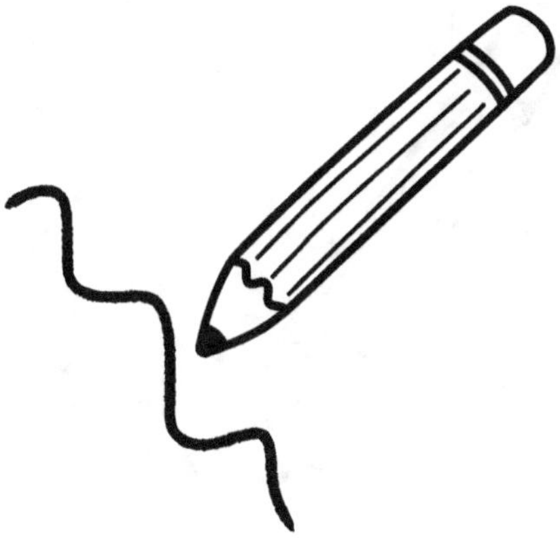

Mom Draws

Child Draws

Sea Lion

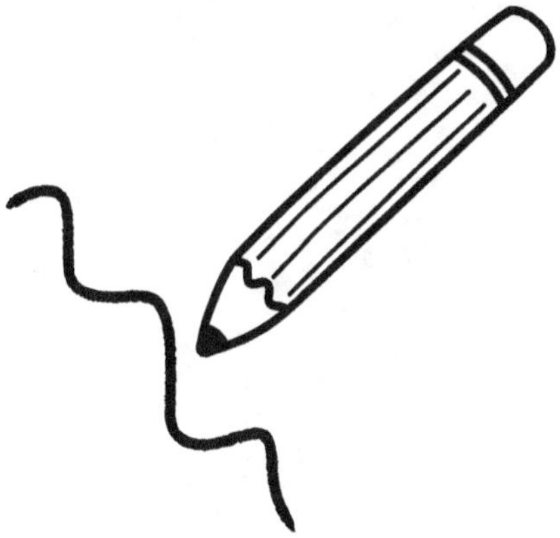

Together

Mom draw a large whale...
Child decorate the whale with
cute hearts...

Together

Child draw 3 cute penguins...
Mom give each penguin a
fun bowtie...

Bee

Butterfly

Dragonfly

Grasshopper

Ladybug

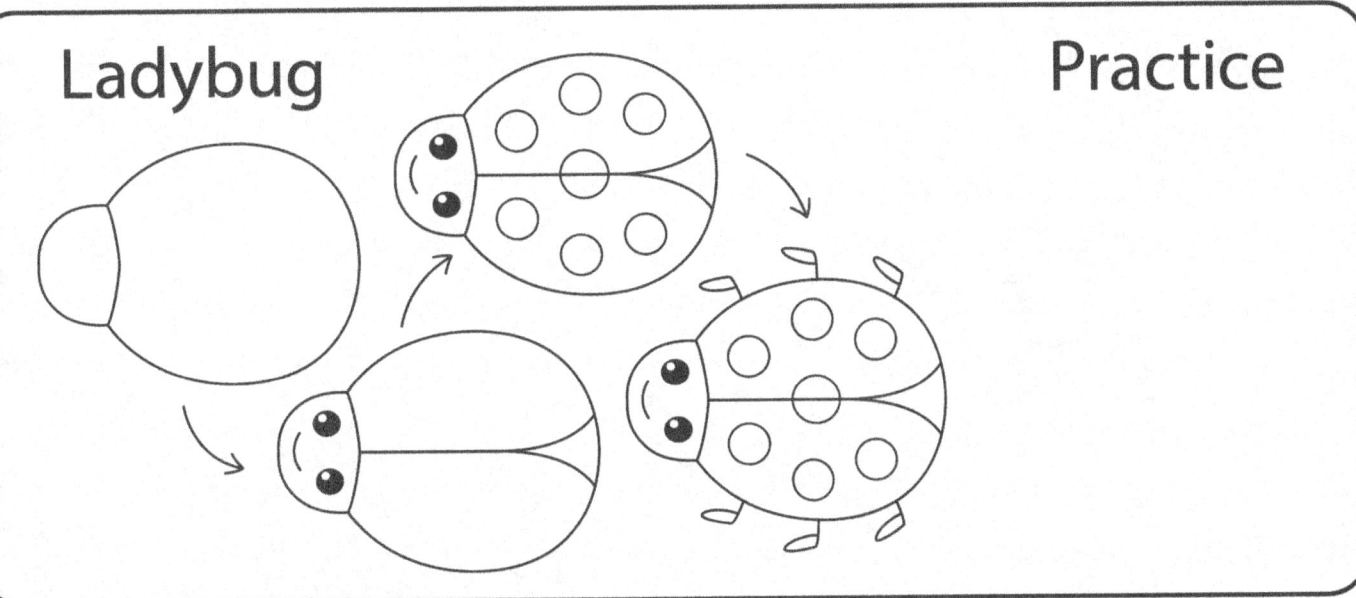

Spider

Mom
Draws

Bee

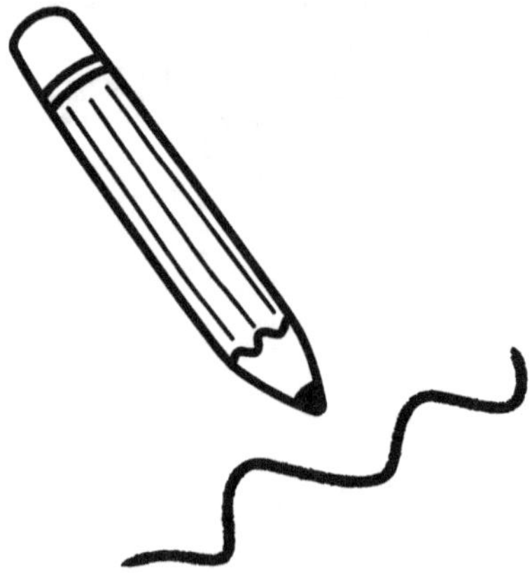

Child

Draws

Mom
Draws

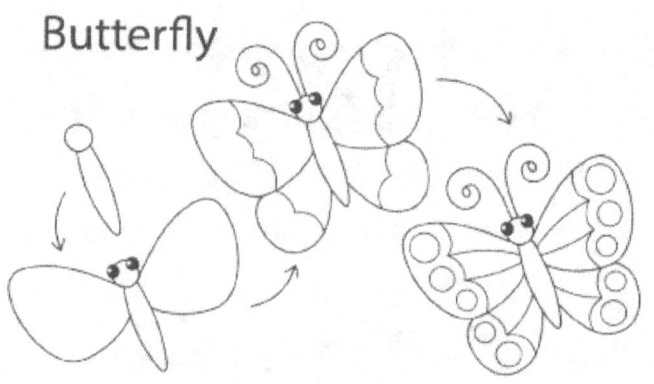

Child
Draws

Butterfly

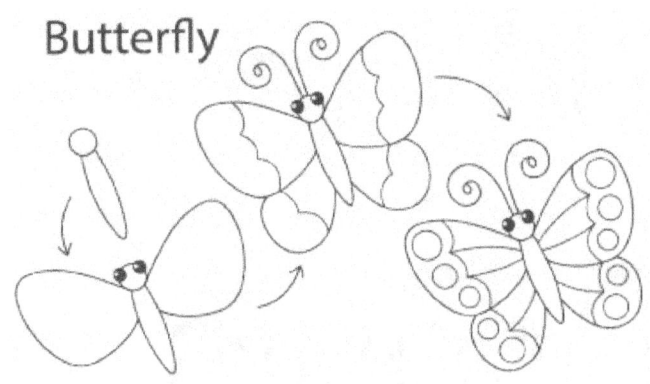

Mom
Draws

Dragonfly

Child
Draws

Dragonfly

Mom Draws

Grasshopper

Child Draws

Grasshopper

Mom Draws

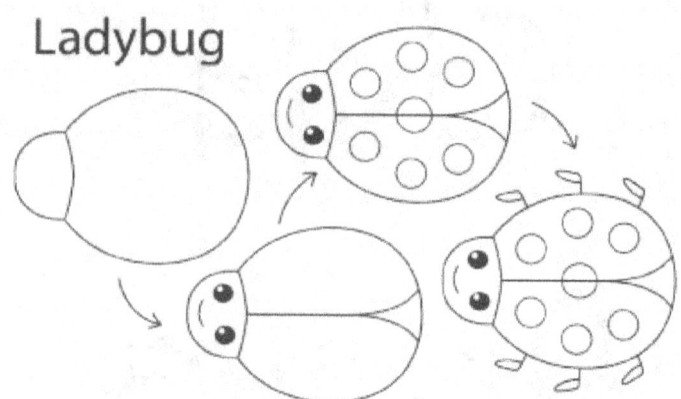

Ladybug

Child Draws

Ladybug

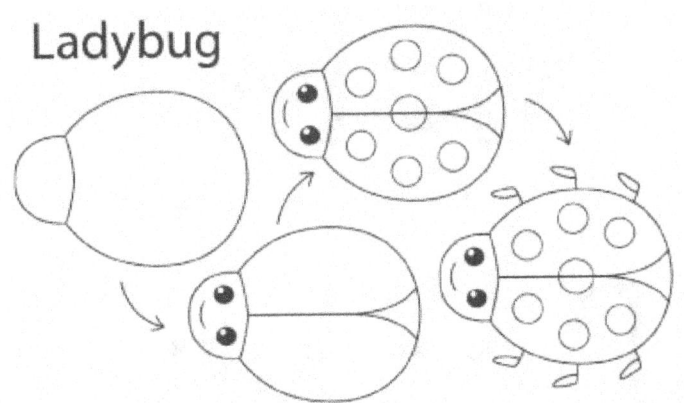

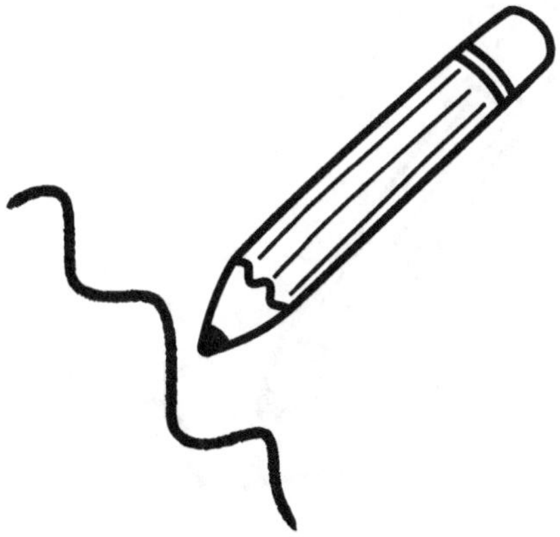

Mom Draws

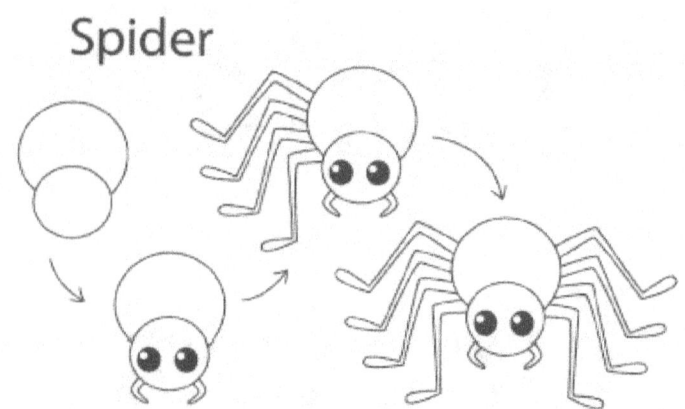

Child

Draws

Spider

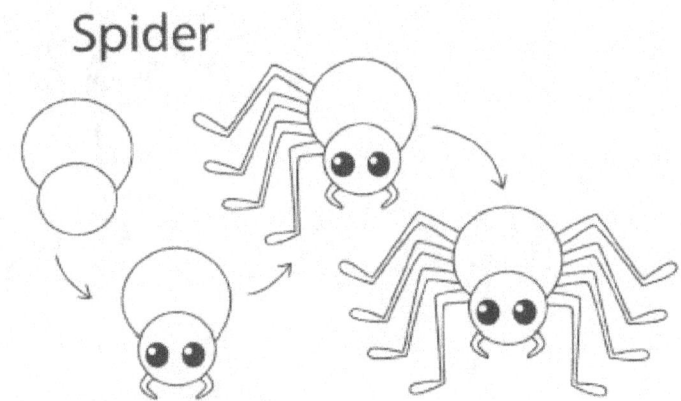

Together

Mom draw beautiful flowers...

Child draw different bugs and insects...

Together

Mom draw a beehive in a tree...

Child draw a bunch of buzzing bees...

Snail

Worm

Snake

Frog Practice

Turtle Practice

Beetle Practice

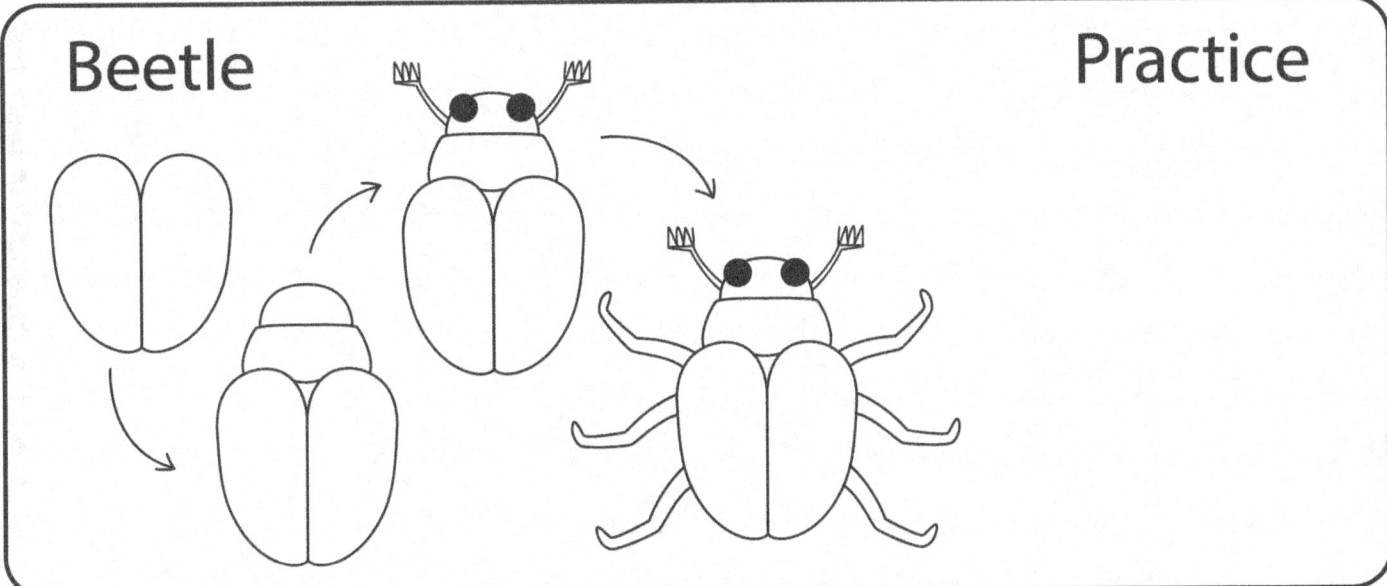

Mom Draws

Snail

Child Draws

Snail

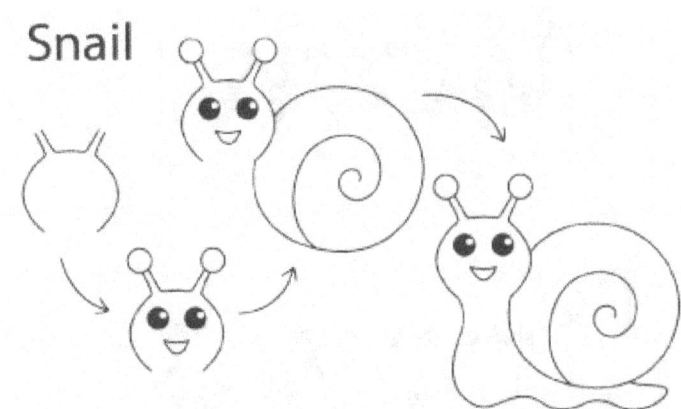

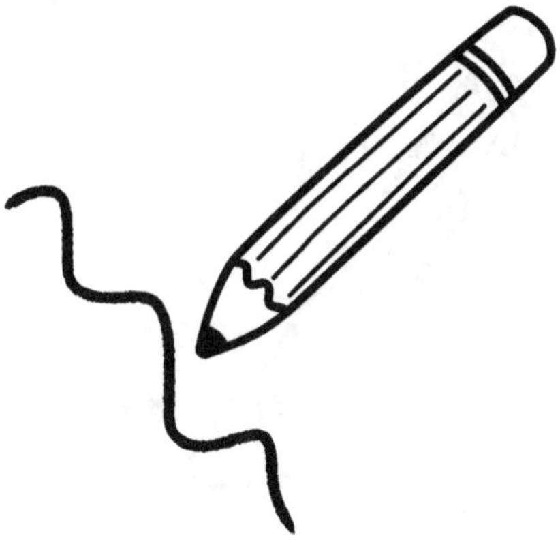

Mom
Draws

Child Draws

Snake

Mom Draws

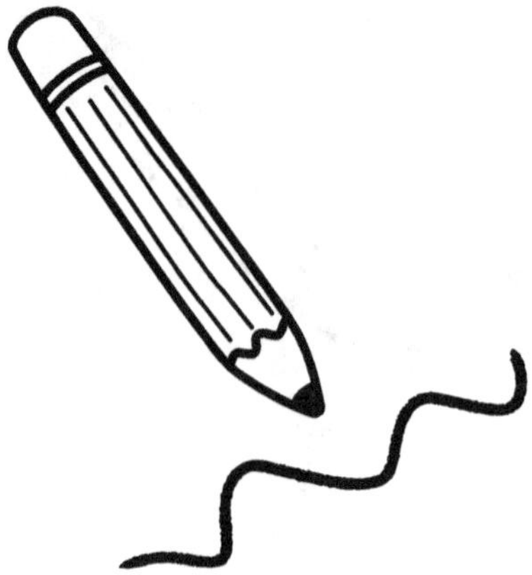

Child
Draws

Frog

Mom Draws

Turtle

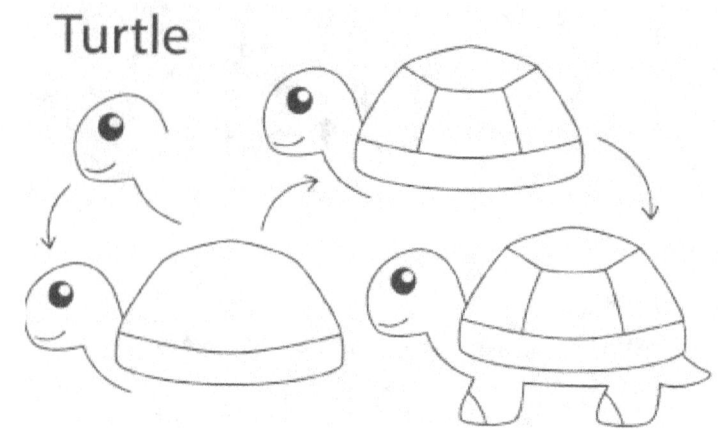

Child Draws

Turtle

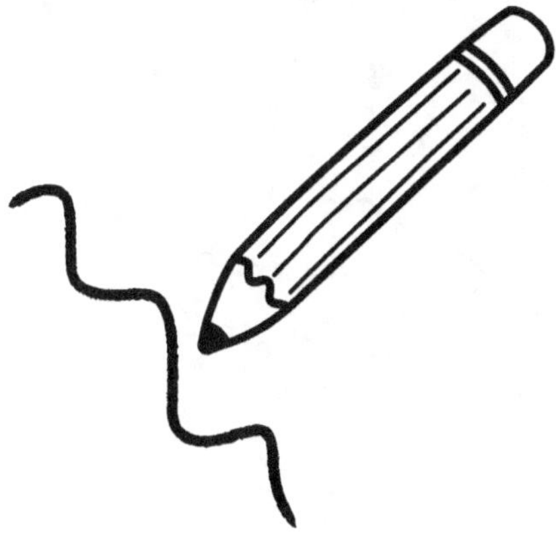

Together

Mom draw a group of lili pads...
Child draw some frogs hopping
on the lili pads...

Together

Mom draw some green turtles...
Child draw some logs and rocks
for the turtles...

FREESTYLE

DRAW YOURSELVES DOING ANYTHING TOGETHER...

Hilarious Kids Games

WOULD YOU
RATHER BOOK
FOR KIDS

Silly EDITION

7.99

HOW TO DRAW ANIMALS FOR KIDS
100 STEP BY STEP DRAWINGS

HOW TO DRAW BOOK FOR KIDS
SIMPLE STEP BY STEP ILLUSTRATIONS FOR DRAWING ANIMALS, MONSTERS, AND CUTE THINGS

HOW TO DRAW BABY ANIMALS FOR KIDS
100 STEP BY STEP ILLUSTRATIONS

HOW TO DRAW MONSTERS FOR KIDS
100 STEP BY STEP ILLUSTRATIONS

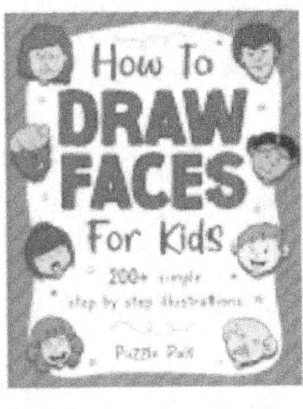

How To DRAW FACES For Kids
200+ simple step by step illustrations

HOW TO DRAW CUTE THINGS FOR KIDS
100 STEP BY STEP ILLUSTRATIONS

HOW TO DRAW CHRISTMAS FOR KIDS
50+ STEP BY STEP DRAWINGS

@puzzlepals_books

puzzlepalsbooks